C. Penny

Victorian Patchwork Patterns

Instructions and Full-Size Templates for 12 Quilts

by Sandra MacDonagh

D1566936

DOVER PUBLICATIONS, INC.

New York

Dedication

To the memory of my grandmother Mary
Bezanson Irish, who taught me to sew; to my
parents, who supported my creations; and to
my daughter Deirdre—may she keep the art of
needlework alive among future generations.

Copyright © 1988 by Sandra MacDonagh.
All rights reserved under Pan American and International
Copyright Conventions.

Published in Canada by General Publishing Company, Ltd.,
30 Lesmill Road, Don Mills, Toronto, Ontario.
Published in the United Kingdom by Constable and Company, Ltd., 10 Orange Street, London WC2H 7EG.

*Victorian Patchwork Patterns: Instructions and Full-Size Templates for 12
Quilts* is a new work, first published by Dover Publications, Inc.,
in 1988.

Manufactured in the United States of America
Dover Publications, Inc., 31 East 2nd Street, Mineola, N.Y.
11501

Library of Congress Cataloging-in-Publication Data

MacDonagh, Sandra.
    Victorian patchwork patterns : instructions and full-size
templates for 12 quilts / by Sandra MacDonagh.
        p.   cm.
    ISBN 0-486-25543-3 (pbk.)
    1. Patchwork—Patterns. 2. Decoration and ornament—
Victorian style. 3. Patchwork quilts. I. Title.
TT835.M258 1988
746.9′7041—dc19   87-28961
                                                         CIP

Introduction

When leisure time permitted, the Victorian housewife kept abreast of the fashionable world through the pages of her ladies' magazines. These publications, famous for their hand-tinted fashion plates, offered songs, poetry, stories and needlework and craft patterns. Many women formed subscription clubs and publishers offered discounted subscription rates to members. In this way, nearly every woman could afford one of these magazines.

The most famous of these ladies' magazines was *Godey's Lady's Book*, established in 1830 by Louis A. Godey of Philadelphia. *Godey's*, edited by Mrs. Sarah Josepha Hale, proved an enormous success and, by 1858, boasted a circulation of 150,000. Louis Godey died in 1878, but the magazine continued publication for another twenty years.

Chief rival to *Godey's* was *Peterson's Magazine*, also published in Philadelphia. Ten years after Godey began his successful *Lady's Book*, Charles Peterson began publishing *Lady's World*. The name was changed, first to *Peterson's Ladies' National Magazine*, then, in 1848, to *Peterson's Magazine*. Its objective was to imitate, underprice and outsell *Godey's*, a goal that was achieved several years after the Civil War when *Peterson's* surpassed a declining *Godey's*. Magazine content was similar to that of *Godey's* and often the same needlework patterns appeared. Peterson published his magazine until his death in 1887. Like *Godey's*, the magazine continued publication until 1898.

A lesser-known Philadelphia magazine, *Ladies' Home Magazine*, began publication in the early 1850s. Timothy S. Arthur owned and edited the magazine until he died in 1885. Again, content was similar to that of *Godey's* and *Peterson's*. Interestingly, Louis Godey held an interest in Arthur's magazine for many years.

Godey's, the first and longest-lasting of these magazines, began to suffer a decline in quality and readership in the 1880s and, by the 1890s, the era of the ladies' magazine was coming to a close.

Early issues of these magazines contained primarily stories and poetry, but, in the 1840s and 1850s, needlework patterns became a popular addition. Numerous forms of popular needlework appeared, among them patterns for patchwork. Pattern illustrations for patchwork bore no titles and only rarely were piecing instructions given. Pincushions, sofa pillows and tablecloths numbered among the suggested uses for patchwork but, strangely enough, its use in bed coverings was often overlooked.

Godey's began offering patchwork in 1851, but the popularity of these patchwork patterns peaked in the mid-1850s—early 1860s. After the latter part of the 1860s, such patterns were rarely featured and patchwork gradually gave way to the extremely popular crazy quilt of the 1880s.

The Victorian era was rich in many types of needlework and unique in patchwork. The patterns featured in the ladies' magazines were intricate allover patterns using small angular pieces that gave a mosaic quality to the finished work. Solid, rich colors were commonly used and the mosaic appearance of the patchwork was heightened by the small patches of many solid shades. Plaids and stripes were popular prints.

Fabrics ranged from piqué and muslin to satin, silk, velvet and brocades, with the richness of the latter fabrics being most popular. Calicos were no longer fashionable and readers were discouraged from using them in their quilts.

Victorian quilts did not usually have borders; instead, the design ran all the way to the edges of the quilt. Angular or scalloped edges were fashionable and many quilts were finished in this way. Occasionally, fringe or a crocheted or knitted edge was added.

From this mosaic-like patchwork, the crazy quilt evolved. Some crazy quilts, labeled "mosaic quilts," contained hundreds of small colorful pieces, giving their maker the opportunity to utilize scraps of every conceivable shape, size and texture. However, many crazy quilts were made solely of satins, silks or velvets. The crazy quilt afforded a woman skilled in embroidery a chance to display her fancy stitching, and favorite motifs frequently adorned patches of the quilt. Thus, the crazy quilt became a much more highly decorative quilt than the patchwork quilts of earlier Victorian days.

On the following pages you will find complete instructions for making 12 full-sized quilts based on designs taken from these ladies' magazines. Full-size templates are given for all of the quilts except the crazy quilt. We have given instructions for making the quilts with straight edges, but the edge pieces can be easily omitted to make a quilt with the shaped edges so beloved by the Victorians.

The patterns in this book span more than 30 years of the Victorian era, from designs featured in the early 1850s, when light-colored fabrics and prints first began giving way to the preference for darker shades, to the crazy quilt of the 1880s, when heavy, rich, dark colors were much in vogue. Through these patterns, the Victorians have left us a glimpse of their concept of beauty and art as well as of their time and place in history.

General Instructions

BUYING AND PREPARING FABRIC

Victorians used everything from velvet, brocade and silk to piqué and muslin in their quilts, but quiltmakers now tend to select cotton or cotton-blend fabrics as being more in accord with today's living. Many Victorian colors and prints are to be found in these fabrics.

Cotton is easier to work with when piecing patchwork, and many quilting "purists" demand it. A cotton blend, however, will long outwear a cotton. If much time and money are to be put into the making of a quilt that will see a lot of use, cotton blends are the better choice.

Yardage has been given for 44"- to 45"-wide fabrics, as they are the most common, but some 36"-wide cottons are still being sold. Check the fabric width before buying and be sure to buy enough additional material if the fabric is less than 44" wide. Many fabric stores have conversion tables and can tell you how much additional yardage is required.

Wash new fabrics to preshrink them and to remove sizing and excess dye that might run after the quilt top is completed. Iron the fabrics before cutting the patches. Check the grain line of the fabric carefully. Lengthwise threads should be parallel to the selvage and crosswise threads exactly perpendicular to the selvage to insure that the patches will be correctly cut. If the fabric seems off-grain, pull it gently to straighten it. Do this on the true bias in the opposite direction to the off-grain edge.

MAKING THE TEMPLATES

All of the pattern pieces needed for the quilts are given as actual-size templates printed on heavy paper at the back of the book. Cut the templates apart, leaving about ⅛" to ¼" margin of paper around, and glue them to lightweight cardboard. Using sharp scissors, a single-edged razor blade or an X-ACTO knife, carefully cut out the templates on the solid lines. These templates include a ¼" seam allowance so the solid outer line is your cutting line and the broken inner line is the sewing line. If desired, you can make a "window" template by cutting out the center of the template on the broken line. In this way you can mark both the cutting line and the sewing line. You must cut the templates carefully, because if they are not accurate, the fabric pieces will not fit together properly. Be careful not to blunt the corners of the templates.

As you use the templates, the edges will begin to wear and the pattern pieces will eventually change their shape. Because of this, it is a good idea to cut duplicate templates from heavy cardboard before beginning to cut your patches. An even better idea is to cut the templates from lightweight plastic. Plastic suitable for templates can be found in any store selling quilting supplies. Lay the cutout cardboard template on the plastic, trace around it with a sharp lead pencil and carefully cut out the plastic template.

CUTTING THE PATCHES

When cutting pattern pieces, the fabric may be opened up or folded over so that more than one patch may be cut at one time. (Note: The yardages given are for cutting the patches with the fabric open. Before folding the fabric, make sure that you will have enough fabric.) Avoid trying to cut too many layers of fabric at once, for this can lead to inaccurate cutting. Fig. 1 illustrates cutting layouts for various pattern shapes. This pattern placement should be followed to obtain the correct number of patches with the yardages given.

To cut the patches, lay the template on the wrong side of the fabric and trace around it using a well-sharpened pencil or tailor's chalk. Trace and cut out all of the patches of each color, then organize the patches according to shape and color as follows: Thread a needle with a 12" strand of thread and knot one end of the thread. As pattern pieces are cut, string like shapes together on the thread (Fig. 2). When a patch of a particular shape is needed, the top piece may be easily lifted off the thread.

PIECING THE QUILT TOP

The intricacy of Victorian patchwork calls for a variety of piecing procedures. Some patterns are easily pieced on the sewing machine while others may require hand sewing. Keep in mind that our Victorian ancestors had the sewing machine, yet many of their quilts were pieced by hand. Follow the piecing instructions given with each individual quilt. Each pattern indicates whether it is more easily pieced by hand or on the sewing machine. Crazy quilts must be sewn by hand.

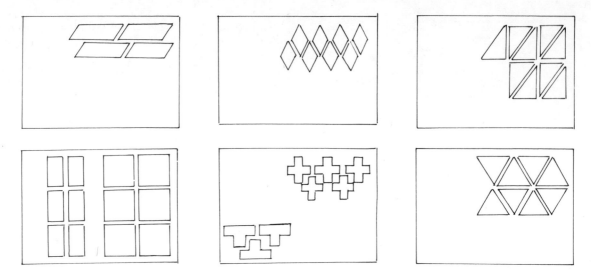

Fig. 1. Sample cutting layouts.

To join two pieces, place them with the right sides together. Pin them together, then stitch exactly on the seam line, being very careful not to stitch into the margins at the corners. If you are sewing by hand, join the pieces with short, simple running stitches *(Fig. 3),* taking a few backstitches at the beginning and end of each seam rather than a knot. After joining two pieces, press the seam allowances to one side, toward the darker fabric *(Fig. 4).* This will keep the seam allowance from showing through light-colored fabrics.

In many of these quilts it will be necessary to set a piece into an angle *(Fig. 5).* Pin the first side of the patch in place. Take a backstitch exactly at the corner, then sew to the edge of the patch, stopping exactly on the seam line *(Fig. 6).* Pin the second side in place, pulling the excess fabric of the bottom piece out of the way, and sew the remainder of the seam *(Fig. 7).*

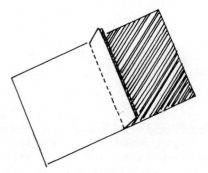

Fig. 4. Press seam allowances toward darker fabric.

Fig. 2. Stringing patches on a thread.

Fig. 3. Running stitch.

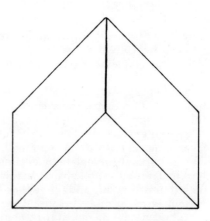

Fig. 5. Triangular patch set into an angle.

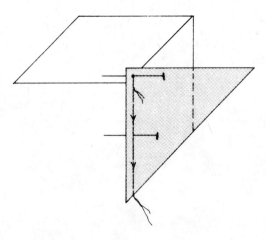

Fig. 6. Pin and sew the first side of the patch.

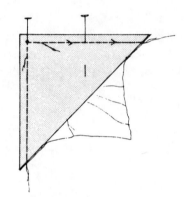

Fig. 7. Sew the second side, pulling the excess fabric out of the way.

FINISHING THE QUILT

Victorian patchwork quilts were unique in their finishing as well as in their piecing. As already mentioned, these quilts rarely had borders and the edges were often left angular or scalloped. Victorian quilts were usually tied or tacked to the lining rather than quilted. Although the ladies' magazines occasionally offered patterns for quilting, these were recommended for use on solid-colored articles, since the quilting stitches did not show up well on the elaborate patchwork of the day. The quilts were quite thin, often using an old, worn blanket or a sheet of flannel as a filler. In some cases, as with crazy quilts, no filler was used at all.

Materials

You will need a soft cotton or cotton-blend fabric to line the quilt. You can use unbleached muslin or you can pick a fabric to harmonize with the quilt top. The lining should be about 2" larger all around than the quilt top; join lengths of fabric to obtain a large enough piece. Press the piece carefully.

For a filler, you can use an old blanket or a flannel sheet as suggested above, or you can use one of the thin dacron polyester quilt battings now available.

You will also need large straight pins, thread for basting, a hand-sewing needle, yarn or embroidery floss and a large-eyed needle for tying the quilt or matching sewing thread for tacking the quilt.

Assembling the Quilt

Press the pieced quilt top very carefully. Spread the lining, wrong side up, on a large flat surface. If you are using a filler, spread it on top of the lining, making sure that there are no lumps or thin places. Fasten the filler to the lining with long basting stitches, starting in the center and working out to the corners and midpoints of the edges. Lay the pressed quilt top, right side up, over the lining and filler, matching the center of the top to the center of the lining and filler. Pin the quilt top in place and baste as before.

To tie the quilt layers together, thread the large-eyed needle with yarn or embroidery floss; do not knot the thread. Pass the needle through the quilt from the top, leaving about 1" of thread on the right side. Bring the needle back up to the right side about ⅛" away; tie the ends of the thread in a knot and trim them to ½". Tie the quilt at the intersections of the seams of the patchwork. To tack the layers together, thread a needle with sewing thread to match the quilt top; do not knot the thread. Insert the needle, through the quilt top only, about 1" away from where you want to tack and bring it back to the surface at the point where you want to make the stitch. Pull the thread gently until the end disappears into the quilt, then take a few small stitches, one on top of the other, through all the layers. Insert the needle through the quilt top only, bringing it out about 1" away; cut the thread close to the surface of the quilt. After the quilt is tied or tacked, remove the basting stitches and trim the backing and filler even with the edges of the quilt.

If the quilt has straight edges, you can bind them with bias binding. You can purchase ready-made bias binding, but it is very simple to make your own from one of the fabrics used in the quilt top. An additional ½ yard of fabric will be needed. Cut and join 1"- to 1¼"-wide bias strips to make a strip long enough to go around the quilt plus a few inches. With the right sides together, pin the strip along the outside edge of the quilt top with the raw edges matching. Overlap the ends of the strip slightly, turning ¼" on the ends to the wrong side of the strip. Sew through all layers ¼" from the edge. Fold the binding over the edges of the quilt to the back, turn under the raw edge and slip-stitch it in place.

If the edges of the quilt are shaped, trim the filler ¼" smaller all around than the quilt top and the lining. Turn the seam allowance on the quilt top and the lining to the inside and slip-stitch the edges together.

Quilt 1 *Size: Approximately 72" by 90".*

This pattern was illustrated in *Godey's Lady's Book* in 1851 and in *Peterson's Magazine* 10 years later.

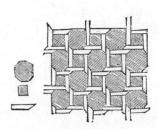

Fabric needed

1½ yds. medium print* for A
2⅞ yds. medium print* for B
2¼ yds. solid for C and D

*For the sample illustrated in color on the covers, the same striped fabric was used for both A and B. The patches were placed with the stripes running horizontally on the A patches and vertically on the B patches.

Number of pieces to cut

Template A—40
Template B—40
Template C—160
Template D—18

Piecing

This pattern can be machine-pieced.

Sew a C strip to one edge of an A patch as in *Fig. 1*. Working counterclockwise, sew a second C strip to the edge of the A patch and the end of the first C strip *(Fig. 2)*. Continue sewing on C strips, sewing the short end of the fourth strip to the extended edge of the first strip *(Fig. 3)*. Sew one B patch to the right-hand edge of this unit and one to the lower edge. Sew C strips to a second A patch as before, then sew this piece below the first B and to the right of the second B to form a unit *(Fig. 4)*.

Make 20 of these units, then assemble them to make the quilt 4 units wide by 5 units long.

To make the edges of this quilt straight, sew D patches along the edges and trim the points of the C strips *(Fig. 5)*. For best results, sew the D patches in place by hand.

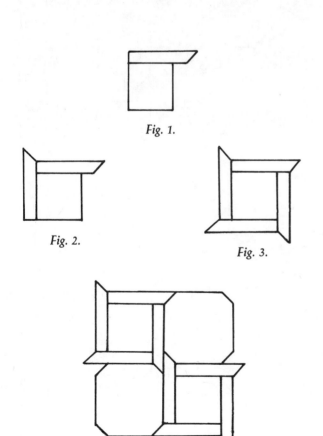

Fig. 1.

Fig. 2.

Fig. 3.

Fig. 4.

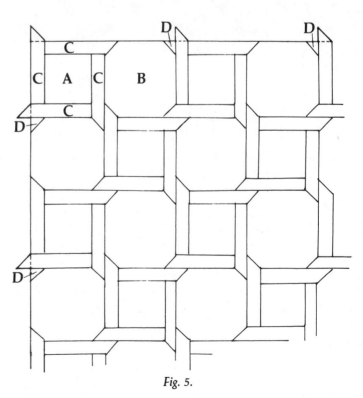

Fig. 5.

Quilt 2

Size: *Approximately 72" by 84".*

☐ Medium solid   ■ Dark solid   ▨ Dark print

10

This popular pattern appeared in *Godey's Lady's Book* twice—first in 1851, then in 1858.

Fabric needed

2½ yds. medium solid for A
2¾ yds. dark solid for B and D
2¾ yds. dark print for C and D

Number of pieces to cut

Template A—224
Template B—215
Template C—216 (turn template over to cut these patches)
Template D—18 from dark solid
Template D—16 from dark print

Piecing

This pattern may be machine-pieced, although care must be taken at the corners.

Sew pieces A, B and C together to form a block *(Fig. 1)*. Make a total of 207 blocks. Following *Fig. 2*, make 9 A/D units, 7 A/D2 units, 8 B/D units and 9 C/D units for the edges. Sew the blocks and edge units together in diagonal rows running upward from left to right *(Fig. 3)* as follows:

Row 1: A/D, 2 blocks, A/D2
Row 2: A/D, 5 blocks, A/D2
Row 3: A/D, 8 blocks, A/D2
Row 4: A/D, 11 blocks, A/D2
Row 5: A/D, 14 blocks, A/D2
Row 6: A/D, 17 blocks, A/D2
Row 7: A/D, 20 blocks, A/D2

Row 8: A/D, 23 blocks
Row 9: A/D, 23 blocks, C/D
Row 10: B/D, 21 blocks, C/D
Row 11: B/D, 18 blocks, C/D
Row 12: B/D, 15 blocks, C/D
Row 13: B/D, 12 blocks, C/D
Row 14: B/D, 9 blocks, C/D
Row 15: B/D, 6 blocks, C/D
Row 16: B/D, 3 blocks, C/D
Row 17: B/D, C/D

Carefully sew the diagonal rows together, pivoting at the corners. Sew the remaining A square into the top left corner and the remaining print D triangle to the top right corner.

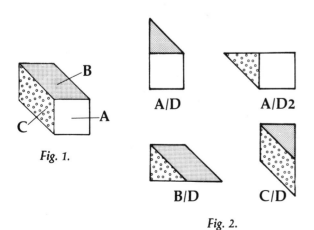

Fig. 1.

Fig. 2.

A/D

A/D2

B/D

C/D

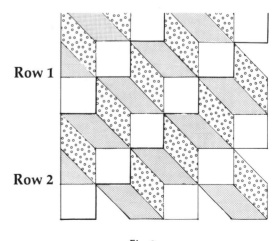

Row 1

Row 2

Fig. 3.

11

Quilt 3

Size: Approximately 77" by 87".

This pattern first appeared in 1851 in *Godey's Lady's Book.* It also became a featured pattern in *Ladies' Home Magazine* in 1860.

Fabric needed

3⅝ yds. print for A
5½ yds. solid for B, C, D and E

Number of pieces to cut

Template A—288
Template B—255
Template C—32
Template D—32
Template E—2
Template E reversed—2 (turn template over to cut these patches)

Piecing

This pattern may be machine-pieced, but care must be taken when sewing the points of B.

Sew an A square to each edge of a B diamond *(Fig. 1)*. Sew a second B diamond to the free adjacent edges of the A squares on the right, then sew A squares to the free edges of this diamond *(Fig. 2)*. Continue across, alternating diamonds and squares until there are 15 B diamonds across; add A squares to the right-hand edge. Make 9 rows in this manner. Join the rows by sewing the free edges of the A squares to B diamonds.

To make the edges straight, insert C and D triangles into the spaces *(Fig. 3)*; sew E patches to the corners.

Fig. 1.

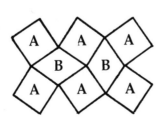

Fig. 2.

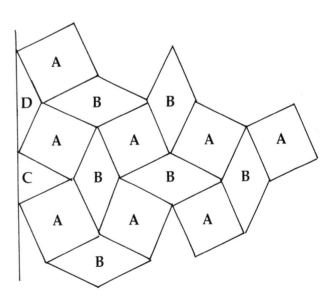

Fig. 3.

Quilt 4 *Size: Approximately 72" by 84".*

Godey's Lady's Book of 1860 featured this pattern.

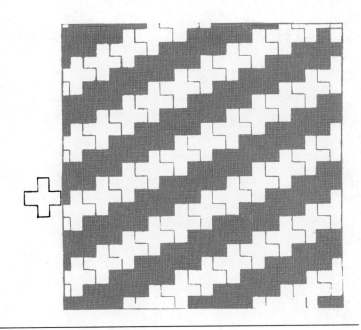

Fabric needed

4⅜ yds. dark
4½ yds. light

Number of pieces to cut

Template A—58 from dark fabric
Template A—57 from light fabric
Template B—13 from dark fabric
Template B—12 from light fabric
Template C—9 from dark fabric
Template C—9 from light fabric

Piecing

This may be pieced on the sewing machine, however, the number of corners in the patch may cause some difficulty. Careful sewing and following the stitching lines exactly should eliminate any machine-piecing problems.

This is a difficult quilt to piece so follow the instructions and diagrams carefully.

Referring to *Fig. 1* for placement, sew the patches together in diagonal rows as follows:

Row 1 (dark fabric): 1 C, 1 A, 1 C, 1 B *(see Fig. 2)*
Row 2 (light fabric): 1 B, 4 A, 1 C, 1 B *(see Fig. 3)*
Row 3 (dark): 1 C, 6 A, 1 C, 1 B
Row 4 (light): 1 B, 9 A, 1 C, 1 B
Rows 5, 7 and 9 (dark): 1 C, 11 A, 1 B
Rows 6, 8 and 10 (light): 1 B, 11 A, 1 C
Row 11 (dark): 3 B *(see Fig. 4)*, 11 A, 1 B
Row 12 (light): 1 B, 1 C, 8 A, 1 C
Row 13 (dark): 1 B, 1 C, 6 A, 1 B
Row 14 (light): 1 B, 1 C, 3 A, 1 C
Row 15 (dark): 1 B, 1 C, 1 A, 1 B

Carefully sew the rows together to form the quilt top. Sew light B squares into the top left and lower right corners.

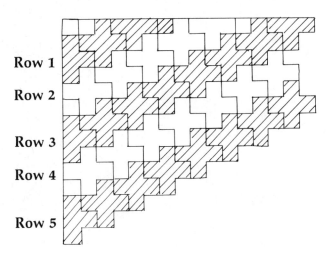

Row 1
Row 2
Row 3
Row 4
Row 5

Fig. 1.

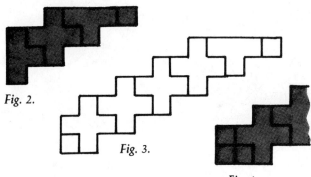

Fig. 2.

Fig. 3.

Fig. 4.

Quilt 5 *Size: Approximately 78" by 90".*

This pattern, submitted by a *Godey's* reader, was printed in an 1864 issue. It is one of the few patterns to include instructions.

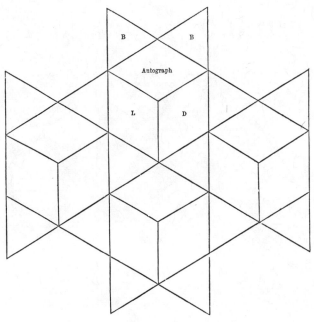

Explanation of the Diagram.—B B for black piece; L for light; D for dark. The remaining blocks are finished in the same manner.

Fabric needed

1¾ yds. white for patches A and E
2 yds. black for patches B and E
dark-colored scraps or 1½ yds. dark fabric for D
light-colored scraps or 1½ yds. light fabric for L

Number of pieces to cut

Template A—162
Template B—324
Template D—163
Template L—163 (turn template over to cut these patches)
Template E—13 from white*
Template E—14 from black*

*These patches are used to give the quilt straight edges and may be omitted.

Piecing:

This pattern may be pieced on a sewing machine.

The patches are assembled into 6" by 90" strips which are joined together to form the quilt top *(Fig. 1)*. Strip 1 begins and ends with the L and D patches and contains 12 A patches. Strip 2 begins with the B patches, ends with the A patch and contains a total of 13 A patches. Make 7 of Strip 1 and 6 of Strip 2. Alternating Strips 1 and 2, sew the strips together, carefully matching the seams.

To give the quilt even edges, sew the white E patches along the top edge and the black E patches along the bottom.

After the quilt is assembled, but before the backing is added, you may have your friends and family sign the white A patches with indelible ink. The signatures can be left as is, or you may embroider over the lines in outline or back stitch.

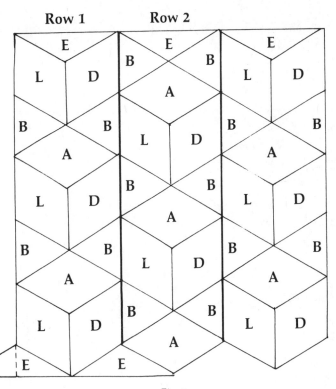

Fig. 1.

17

Quilt 6 *Size: Approximately 72" by 84".*

This pattern was featured in an 1859 issue of *Godey's Lady's Book*.

Fabric needed

4 yds. dark
4 yds. light

Number of pieces to cut

Template A—84 from each fabric
Template B—84 from each fabric

Piecing

This pattern may be pieced on the sewing machine.

The quilt top is composed of 42 twelve-inch blocks. To make the block, sew a dark A patch to a light B patch *(Fig. 1)*. Repeat to make 4 units. Sew the units together in pairs *(Fig. 2)*, then sew the pairs together to complete the block. Make 21 blocks like this, and 21 blocks using light A patches and dark B patches.

Alternating the blocks, sew them together *(Fig. 3)* to make a quilt top 6 blocks wide by 7 blocks long.

Although the Victorians rarely added borders to their quilts, a border could be added to this pattern to give it a more finished look. The pattern would also be attractive made with all of the A patches in one fabric and the B patches in another. This would bring out the star and diamond design *(Fig. 4)*. For this combination, you would need 5 yds. of fabric for A and 3 yds. for B.

Fig. 1.

Fig. 2.

Fig. 3.

Fig. 4.

Quilt 7 *Size: Approximately 82" by 92".*

In 1862, *Godey's Lady's Book* featured this one-patch pattern.

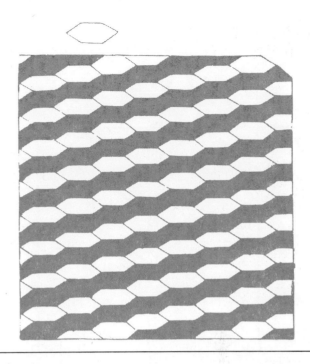

Fabric needed

5 yds. striped fabric
5 yds. solid fabric

Number of pieces to cut

Template A—141 from each fabric
Template B*—23 from striped fabric
Template B*—24 from solid fabric

*These patches are used to give the quilt straight edges and may be omitted.

Piecing

The patches can be easily sewn into vertical strips on the sewing machine. While the strips can be sewn together by machine, those who find sewing angles and points on the machine difficult may wish to sew them by hand.

This quilt consists of 12 vertical strips of A patches in alternating fabrics. Strip 1 begins with a solid patch and contains 23 patches. Strip 2 begins with a solid patch and contains 24 patches. Strip 3 begins with a striped patch and contains 23 patches. Strip 4 begins with a striped patch and contains 24 patches. Repeat this sequence twice more. Carefully sew the strips together.

To give the quilt straight edges, sew the B patches along the side edges, then trim the top and bottom edges as shown by the broken line in *Fig. 1.*

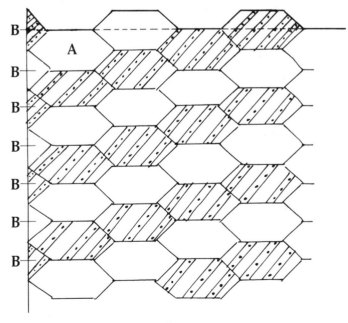

Fig. 1.

Quilt 8

Size: Approximately 84" by 88".

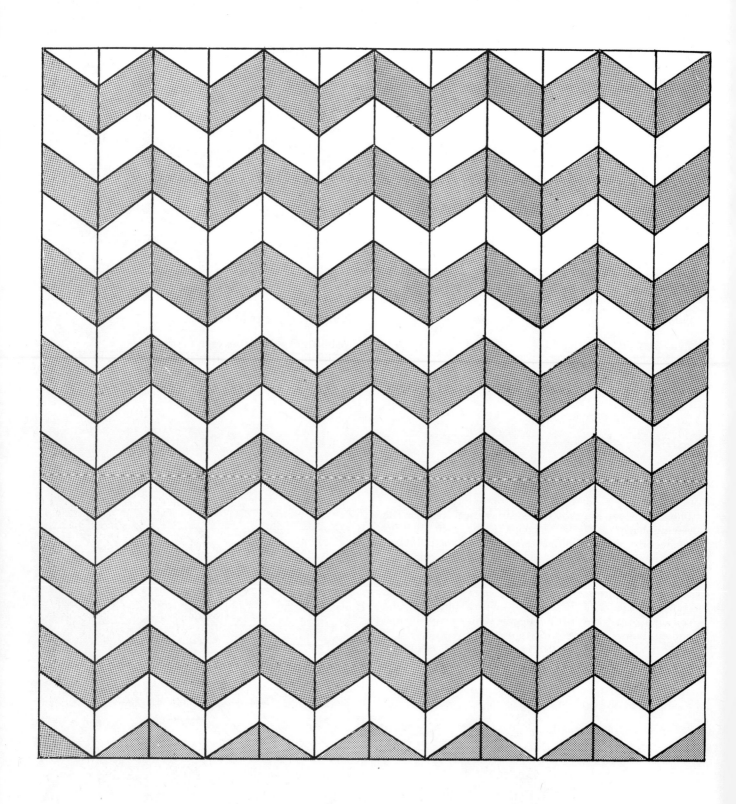

This popular one-patch pattern was illustrated by *Godey's* in two different years prior to a *Peterson's Magazine* illustration in 1861. Two of these illustrations show the pattern with the zigzag stripes running up and down the quilt and pointed side edges. The third shows the stripes running across the quilt as presented here.

Fabric needed

4 yds. of dark fabric
4 yds of light fabric

Number of pieces to cut

Template A—42 from each fabric
Template B—42 from each fabric (turn template over to cut these patches)
Template C*—6 from each fabric
Template D*—6 from each fabric (turn template over to cut these patches)

*These patches are used to give the quilt straight edges and may be omitted.

Piecing

This pattern lends itself to easy machine-piecing.

The patches are assembled into 12 vertical strips which are then sewn together to form the quilt top. Begin by sewing a row of A patches together, alternating light and dark *(Fig. 1)*. The completed strip should have 7 patches of each fabric. If you want the quilt to have straight edges, sew a C patch to the top and the bottom of the strip. Being careful to start with the same color patch as in the A strip, sew a row of B patches together in the same way. Add D patches to straighten the edges if desired. Make 6 strips each of A and B patches, then sew them together alternating the strips *(Fig. 2)*.

Fig. 1.

Fig. 2.

23

Quilt 9

Size: Approximately 54" by 72".

This pattern appeared in the 1851 *Godey's Lady's Book*.

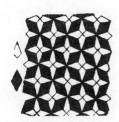

Fabric needed

2¼ yds. dark fabric for patch A
multicolored scraps to equal 4¾ yds. for patch B

Number of pieces to cut

Template A—432
Template B—906 (all of the points of a single star should
   be cut from the same color fabric, so you may wish to
   cut the pieces for each star as you go).

Piecing

For best results, this pattern should be sewn together by
hand.

   Sew two B patches together along one short diagonal
edge *(Fig. 1)*. Repeat with two more patches. Sew the two
pairs together to form a star *(Fig. 2)*. Make 196 stars.
Following *Fig. 3*, make 38 three-quarter stars for the
edges; make 4 half-stars for the corners. Assemble the
quilt top by sewing the stars to the A diamonds *(Fig. 4)*.
Continue joining the stars until the quilt top is 9 stars
wide and 12 stars long. Sew the three-quarter stars in
place along the edges and the half-stars to the corners.
Trim the edges as shown by the broken lines in *Fig. 4*.

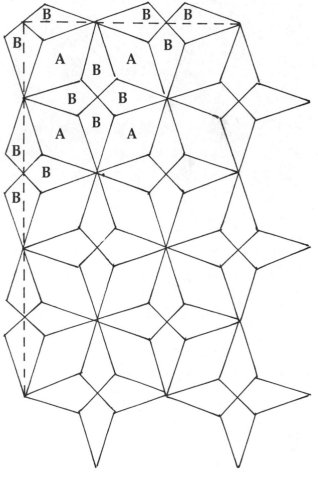

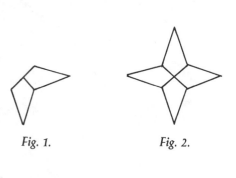

Fig. 1.   Fig. 2.

Fig. 3.

Fig. 4.

Quilt 10

Size: Approximately 77" by 92".

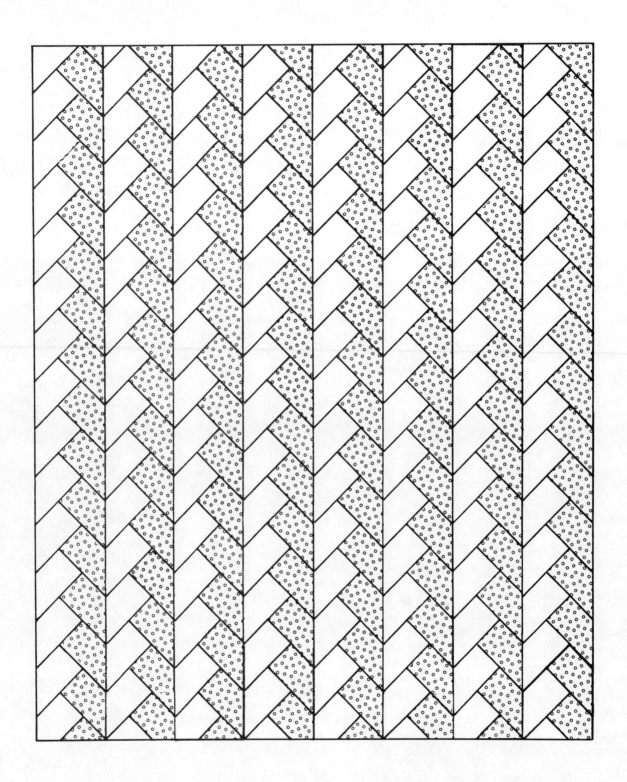

The readers of *Peterson's Magazine* were offered this patchwork pattern in 1862.

Fabric needed

3¾ yds. solid A
3¾ yds. print for B

Number of pieces to cut

Template A—112 (turn template over to cut these patches)
Template B—112
Template C*—4 from each fabric
Template D*—4 from each fabric
Template E*—4 from each fabric

*These patches are used to give the quilt straight edges and may be omitted.

Piecing

This pattern may be pieced on the sewing machine.

The patches are assembled into 8 vertical strips which are then joined to complete the quilt top. Beginning at the bottom of Strip 1, sew a print E patch to an A patch as in *Fig. 1*. Sew the long edge of a B patch to the long straight edge of this piece *(Fig. 2)*, then sew the long edge of an A patch to the edge of the piece. Continue in this way, alternating A and B patches, until there are 14 of each patch in the strip. Sew a print C patch to the top right corner of the strip and a solid D patch to the top left corner *(Fig. 3)*. Trim off the point at the bottom of the strip.

For strip 2, sew a solid E patch to a B patch as in *Fig. 4;* then sew an A patch to this piece *(Fig. 5)*. Continue as for Strip 1, sewing a print D patch to the top right corner and a solid C patch to the top left corner of the strip.

Make 4 of each strip. Carefully matching the points of the patches, sew the strips together, alternating Strip 1 and Strip 2.

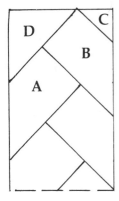

Fig. 3.

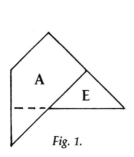

Fig. 1.

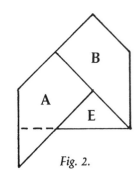

Fig. 2.

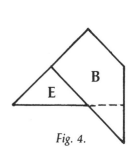

Fig. 4.

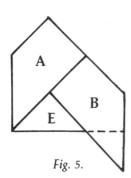

Fig. 5.

Quilt 11 *Size: Approximately 81" by 94".*

This pattern appeared in *Godey's Lady's Book* in 1851.

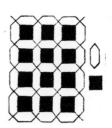

Fabric needed

2¾ yds. dark floral print or solid for A
7 yds. medium solid for B, C and D

Number of pieces to cut

Template A—168
Template B—362
Template C*—48
Template D*—4

*These patches are used to give the quilt straight edges and may be omitted.

Piecing

This pattern may be pieced on the sewing machine, although extra care must be taken when sewing the corners of the A patches and the ends of the B patches.

Sew a B patch to each of the 4 sides of an A patch; sew the short diagonal edges of these B patches together *(Fig. 1)*. Sew another A patch to the free edge of one of the patches *(Fig. 2)*; sew B patches to the remaining free edges of this A patch. Continue in this way, alternating A and B patches, until you have a row of 12 A patches surrounded by B patches.

To begin the 2nd row, sew B patches to 3 sides only of the first A patch (the remaining edge of the A patch will be sewn to the lower edge of the row above). Continue as for the first row, omitting the B patches along the top edge *(Fig. 3)*.

Make a total of 14 rows, then sew the rows together, pivoting carefully at the points and corners.

To give the quilt top straight edges, insert C and D patches along the edges as shown in *Fig. 4*.

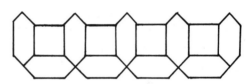

Fig. 3.

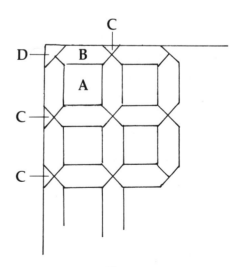

Fig. 4.

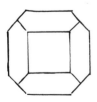

Fig. 1.

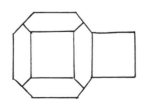

Fig. 2.

Quilt 12

In the 1880s crazy work became very popular. Magazines of the period frequently mentioned the crazy quilt offering hints and suggestions, but no illustrations were given.

Many consider the crazy quilt to be the easiest of all quilts to piece. A foundation fabric, a bag of scraps and embroidery floss will be needed for making a crazy quilt.

Select a foundation fabric such as unbleached muslin or a bed sheet of the appropriate size. Preshrink and iron this fabric. If necessary, piece and sew the fabric to make a foundation piece of the desired size. Remember, the quilt will be the size of the foundation fabric.

Crazy-quilt patches may be scraps of any shape, size, texture and color. Very large scraps may be cut down to make several smaller pieces. Scraps having a straight edge should be set aside to use when a piece is needed along an edge of the quilt. Crazy-quilt patches should be fitted together as a puzzle, trimming the fabric only when necessary.

Begin piecing in one corner. If possible, find a scrap having a right angle and place that patch in the corner. If necessary, a patch may be trimmed to the correct shape.

Sewing through all thicknesses, baste this patch to the corner of the foundation fabric. Sew along the straight edges of this patch, leaving the other two sides free to turn over the edge of the piece that will be placed next to it *(Fig. 1)*.

Select the patches that will go next to the corner piece and pin them in place, allowing for a ½" overlap *(Fig. 2)*. Turn under the ¼" seam allowance on the overlapping edge of the first patch *(Fig. 3)* and baste it in place. Continue to arrange, pin and baste the other patches in place. Make sure the foundation fabric remains smooth and does not pucker as the patches are basted into place.

Using embroidery floss, begin the decorative stitching (through all layers) along the edges of the patches *(Fig. 4)*. When the edges are secured by the embroidery, the basting stitches may be removed. Feather, buttonhole, fern, herringbone, chevron and wheat-ear stitches are commonly used to decorate crazy work *(Fig. 5)*. Pictures of flowers or favorite motifs may be embroidered on the patches.

Crazy quilts do not contain a filler. Line and bind the quilt top as with any other quilt. Tie the top and lining together.

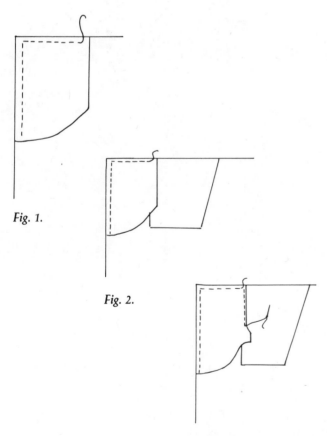

Fig. 1.

Fig. 2.

Fig. 3.

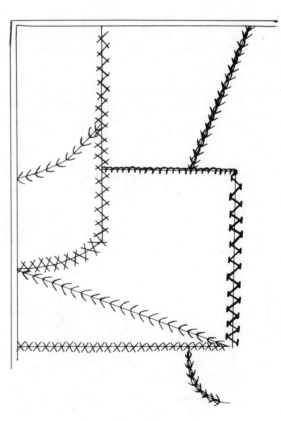

Fig. 4.

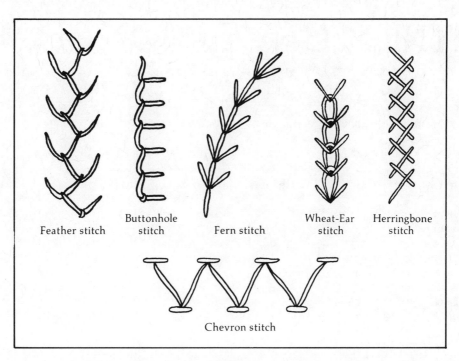

Feather stitch   Buttonhole stitch   Fern stitch   Wheat-Ear stitch   Herringbone stitch

Chevron stitch

Fig. 5.

METRIC CONVERSION CHART

CONVERTING INCHES TO CENTIMETERS AND YARDS TO METERS

mm — millimeters   cm — centimeters   m — meters

INCHES INTO MILLIMETERS AND CENTIMETERS
(Slightly rounded off for convenience)

inches	mm		cm	inches	cm	inches	cm	inches	cm
⅛	3mm			5	12.5	21	53.5	38	96.5
¼	6mm			5½	14	22	56	39	99
⅜	10mm	or	1cm	6	15	23	58.5	40	101.5
½	13mm	or	1.3cm	7	18	24	61	41	104
⅝	15mm	or	1.5cm	8	20.5	25	63.5	42	106.5
¾	20mm	or	2cm	9	23	26	66	43	109
⅞	22mm	or	2.2cm	10	25.5	27	68.5	44	112
1	25mm	or	2.5cm	11	28	28	71	45	114.5
1¼	32mm	or	3.2cm	12	30.5	29	73.5	46	117
1½	38mm	or	3.8cm	13	33	30	76	47	119.5
1¾	45mm	or	4.5cm	14	35.5	31	79	48	122
2	50mm	or	5cm	15	38	32	81.5	49	124.5
2½	65mm	or	6.5cm	16	40.5	33	84	50	127
3	75mm	or	7.5cm	17	43	34	86.5		
3½	90mm	or	9cm	18	46	35	89		
4	100mm	or	10cm	19	48.5	36	91.5		
4½	115mm	or	11.5cm	20	51	37	94		

YARDS TO METERS
(Slightly rounded off for convenience)

yards	meters	yards	meters	yards	meters	yards	meters	yards	meters
⅛	0.15	2⅛	1.95	4⅛	3.80	6⅛	5.60	8⅛	7.45
¼	0.25	2¼	2.10	4¼	3.90	6¼	5.75	8¼	7.55
⅜	0.35	2⅜	2.20	4⅜	4.00	6⅜	5.85	8⅜	7.70
½	0.50	2½	2.30	4½	4.15	6½	5.95	8½	7.80
⅝	0.60	2⅝	2.40	4⅝	4.25	6⅝	6.10	8⅝	7.90
¾	0.70	2¾	2.55	4¾	4.35	6¾	6.20	8¾	8.00
⅞	0.80	2⅞	2.65	4⅞	4.50	6⅞	6.30	8⅞	8.15
1	0.95	3	2.75	5	4.60	7	6.40	9	8.25
1⅛	1.05	3⅛	2.90	5⅛	4.70	7⅛	6.55	9⅛	8.35
1¼	1.15	3¼	3.00	5¼	4.80	7¼	6.65	9¼	8.50
1⅜	1.30	3⅜	3.10	5⅜	4.95	7⅜	6.75	9⅜	8.60
1½	1.40	3½	3.20	5½	5.05	7½	6.90	9½	8.70
1⅝	1.50	3⅝	3.35	5⅝	5.15	7⅝	7.00	9⅝	8.80
1¾	1.60	3¾	3.45	5¾	5.30	7¾	7.10	9¾	8.95
1⅞	1.75	3⅞	3.55	5⅞	5.40	7⅞	7.20	9⅞	9.05
2	1.85	4	3.70	6	5.50	8	7.35	10	9.15

AVAILABLE FABRIC WIDTHS

25″	65cm	50″	127cm
27″	70cm	54″/56″	140cm
35″/36″	90cm	58″/60″	150cm
39″	100cm	68″/70″	175cm
44″/45″	115cm	72″	180cm
48″	122cm		

AVAILABLE ZIPPER LENGTHS

4″	10cm	10″	25cm	22″	55cm
5″	12cm	12″	30cm	24″	60cm
6″	15cm	14″	35cm	26″	65cm
7″	18cm	16″	40cm	28″	70cm
8″	20cm	18″	45cm	30″	75cm
9″	22cm	20″	50cm		

QUILT #1
Template A

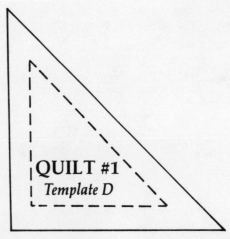

QUILT #1
Template D

PLATE 1

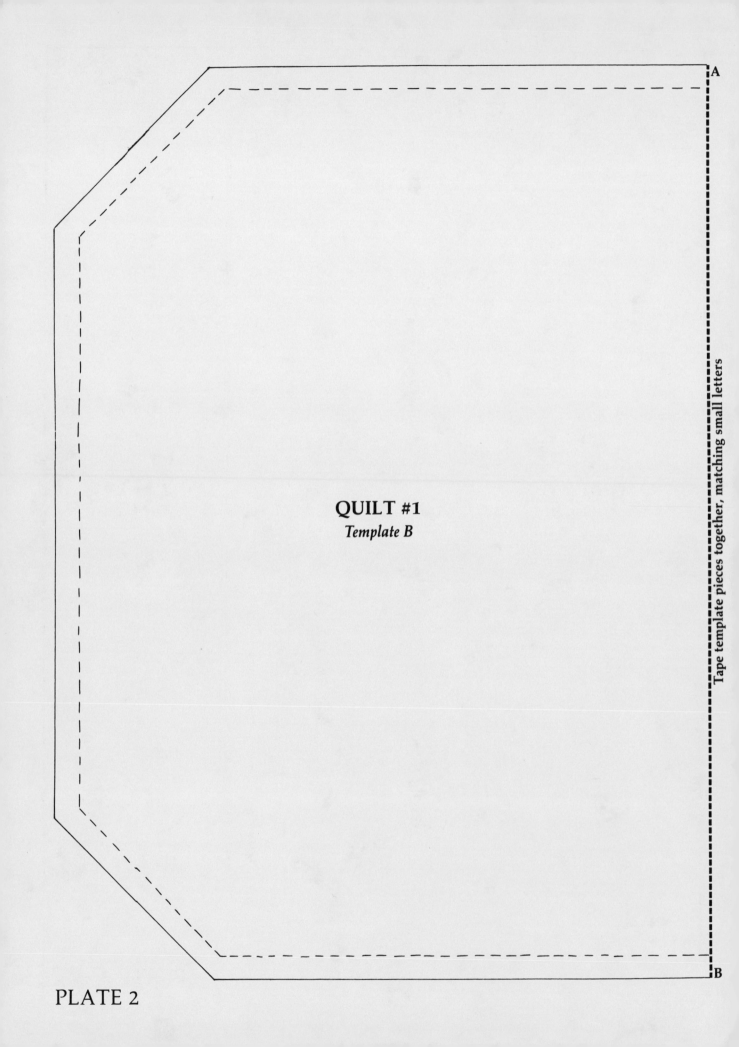

A

QUILT #1
Template B

Tape template pieces together, matching small letters

B

PLATE 2

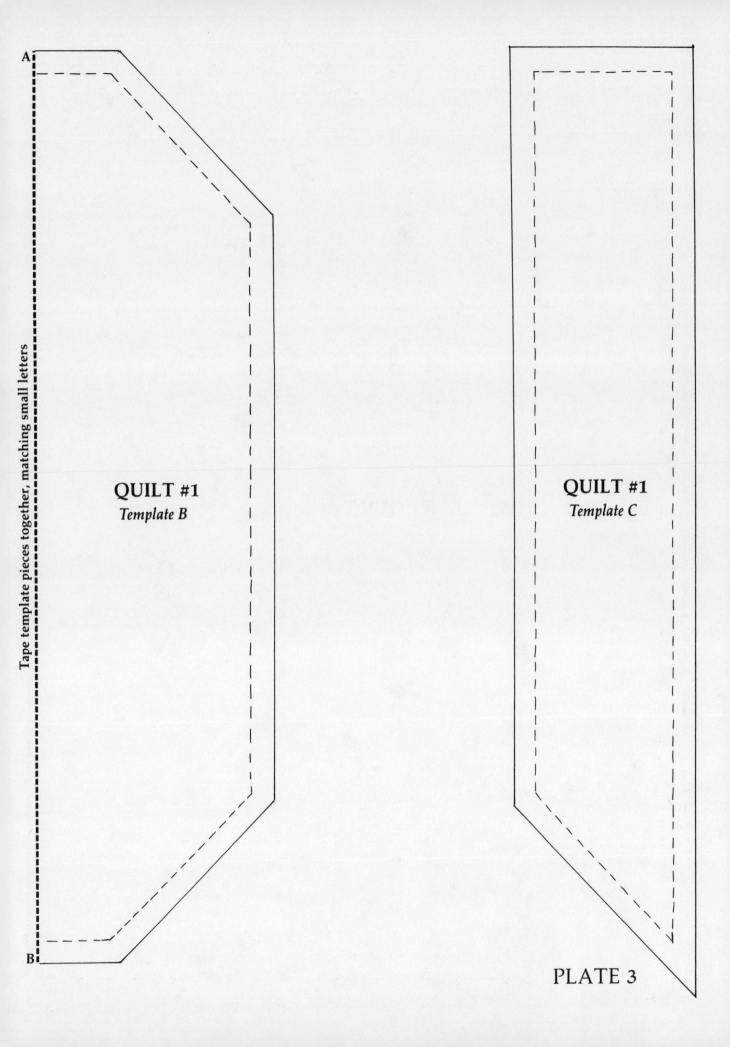

A

Tape template pieces together, matching small letters

QUILT #1
Template B

B

QUILT #1
Template C

PLATE 3

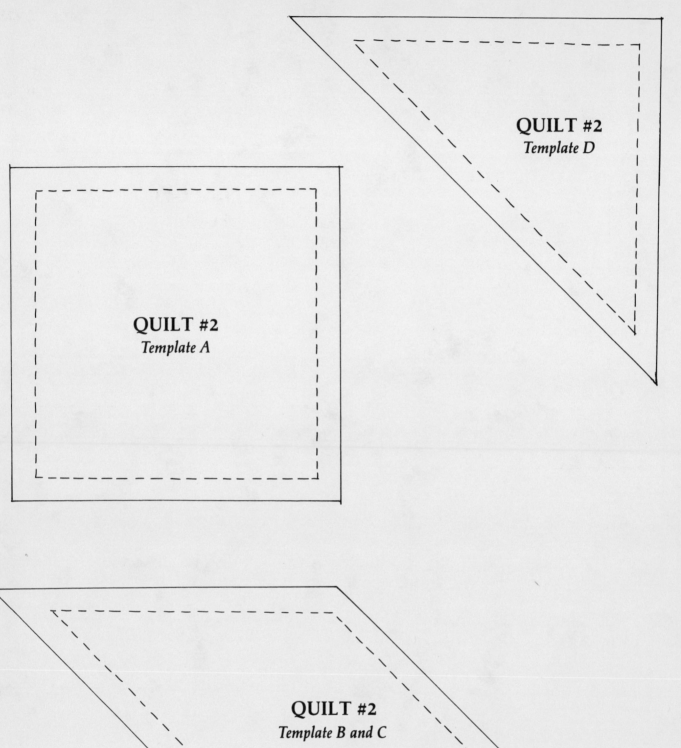

QUILT #2
Template D

QUILT #2
Template A

QUILT #2
Template B and C
Turn template over to cut C patches

PLATE 4

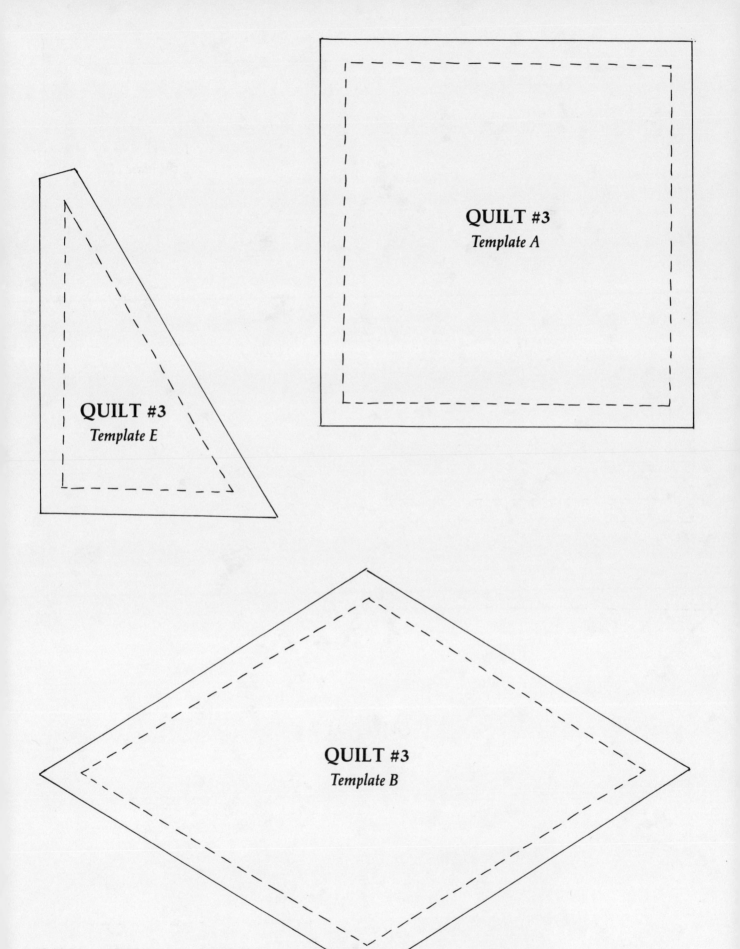

QUILT #3
Template E

QUILT #3
Template A

QUILT #3
Template B

PLATE 5

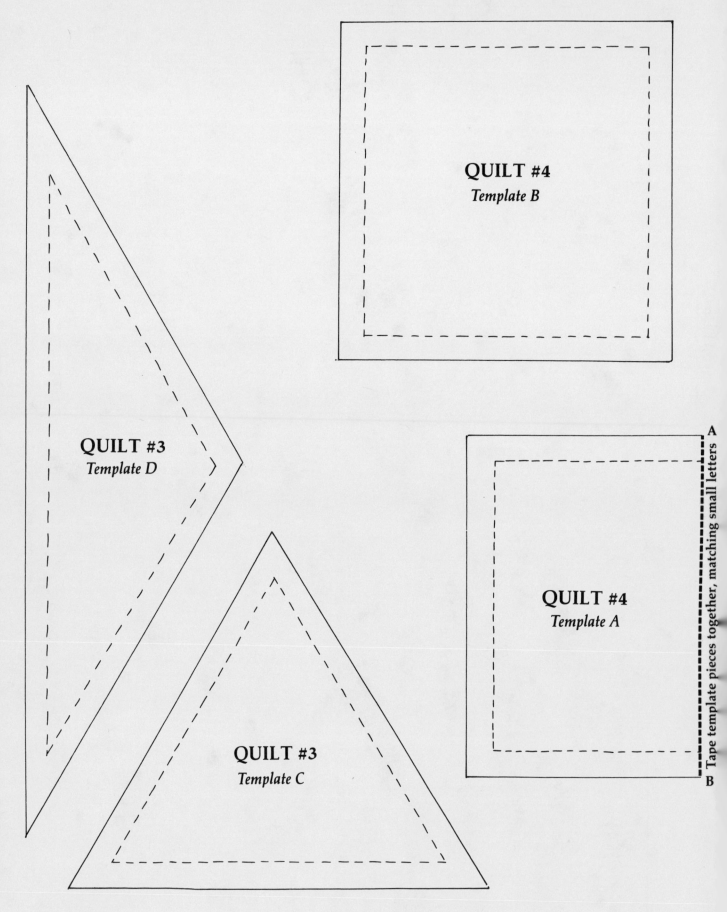

QUILT #4
Template B

QUILT #3
Template D

A

Tape template pieces together, matching small letters

QUILT #4
Template A

QUILT #3
Template C

B

PLATE 6

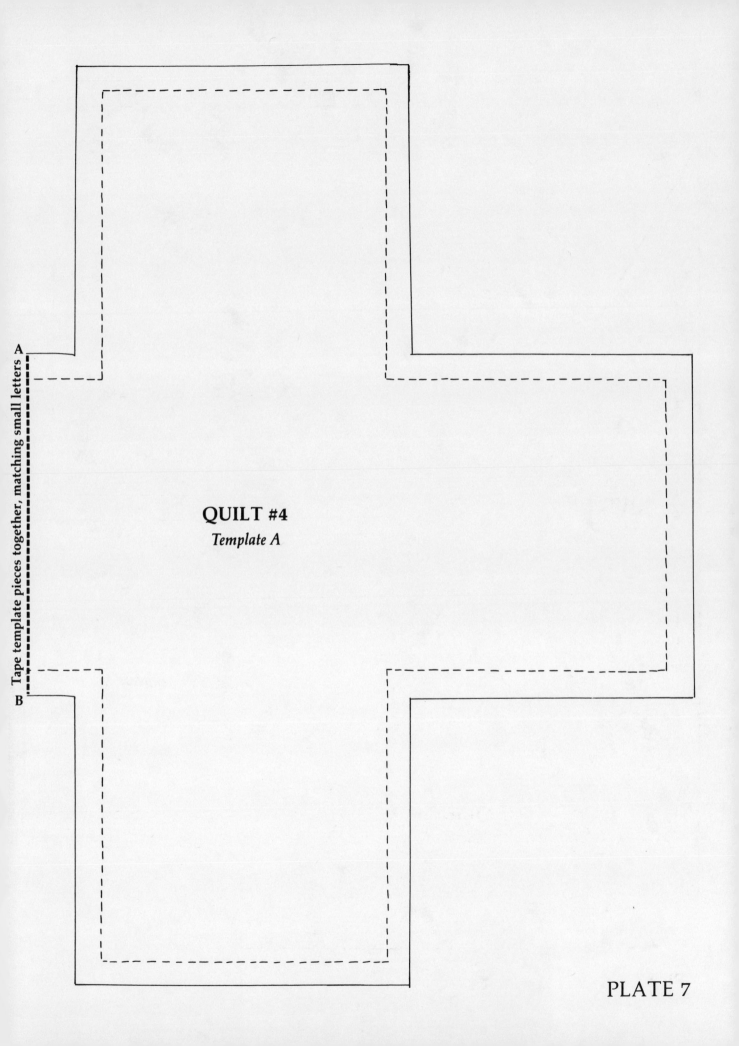

A

Tape template pieces together, matching small letters

B

QUILT #4

Template A

PLATE 7

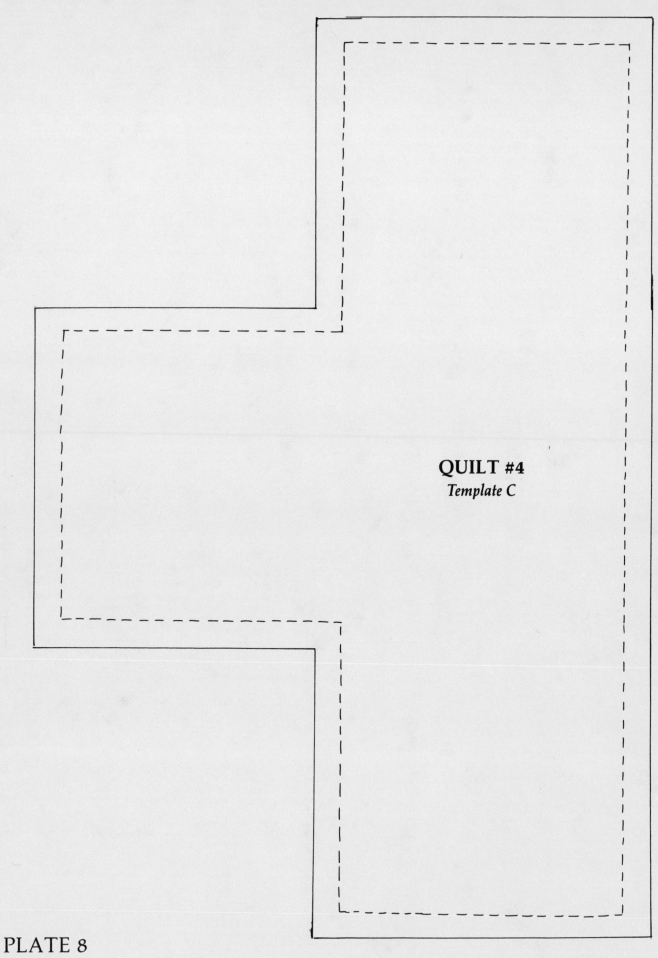

QUILT #4
Template C

PLATE 8

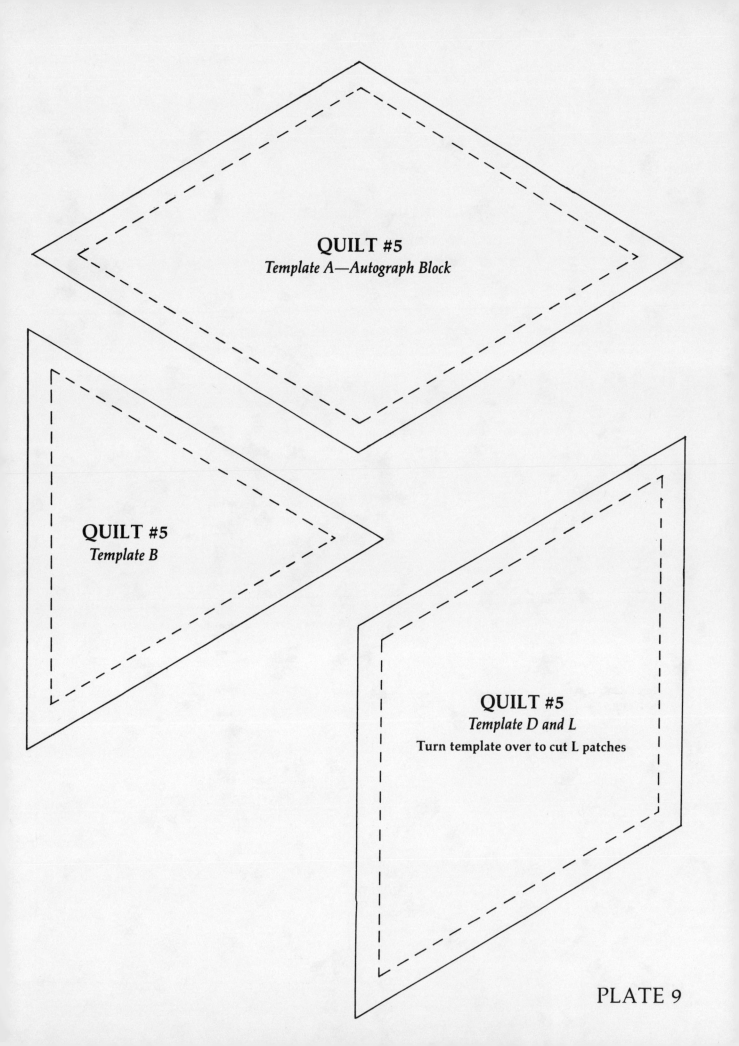

QUILT #5
Template A—Autograph Block

QUILT #5
Template B

QUILT #5
Template D and L
Turn template over to cut L patches

PLATE 9

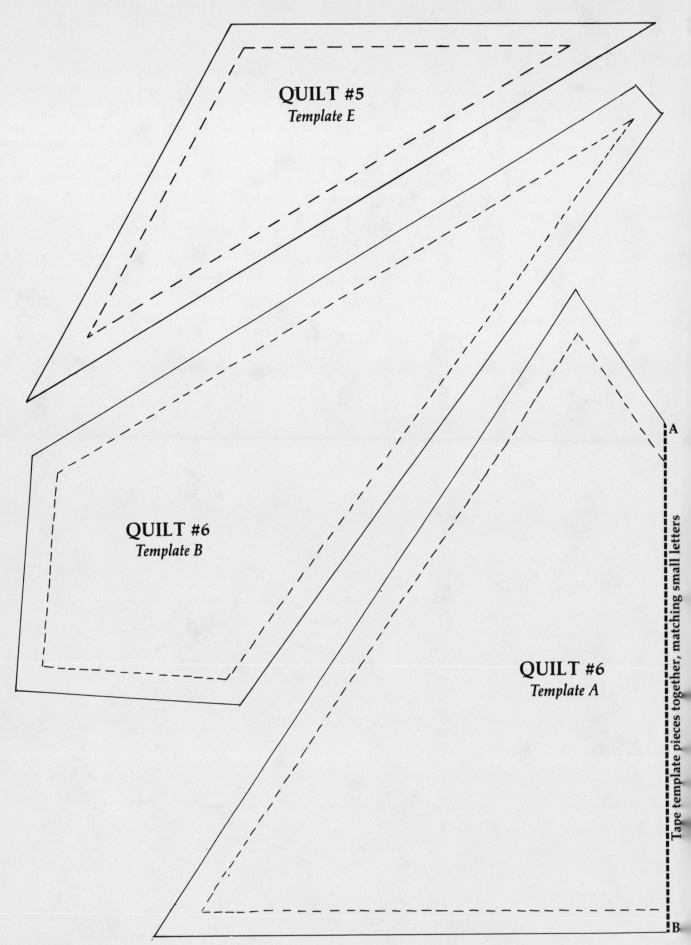

QUILT #5
Template E

QUILT #6
Template B

QUILT #6
Template A

A

B

Tape template pieces together, matching small letters

PLATE 10

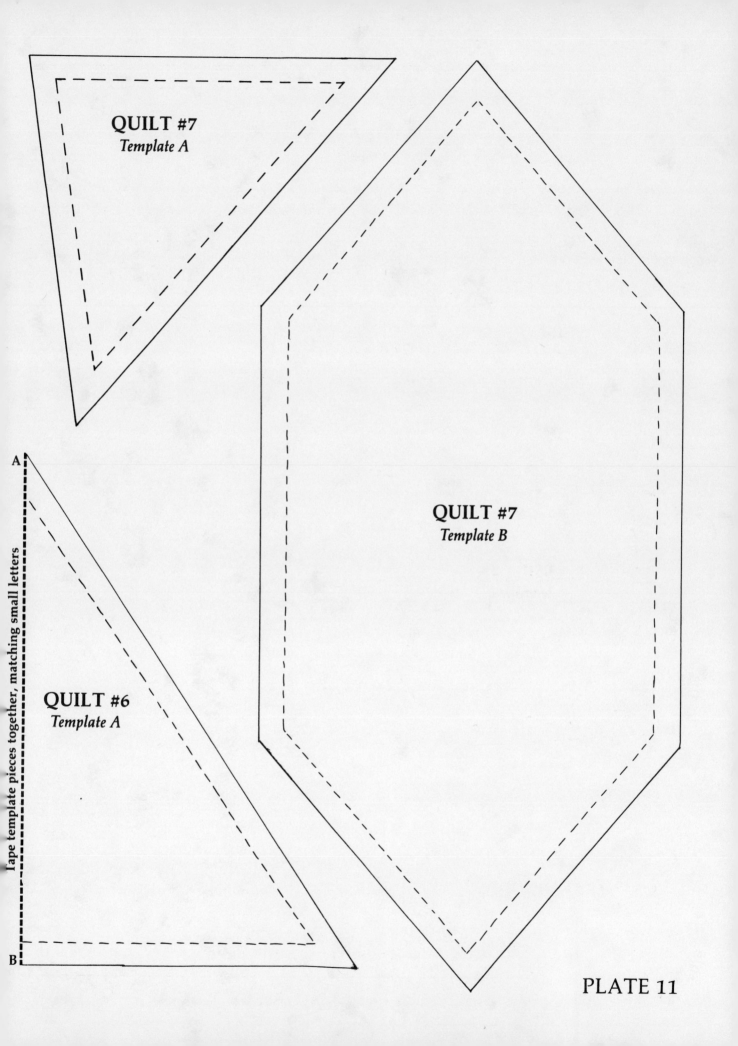

QUILT #7
Template A

QUILT #7
Template B

Tape template pieces together, matching small letters

A

B

QUILT #6
Template A

PLATE 11

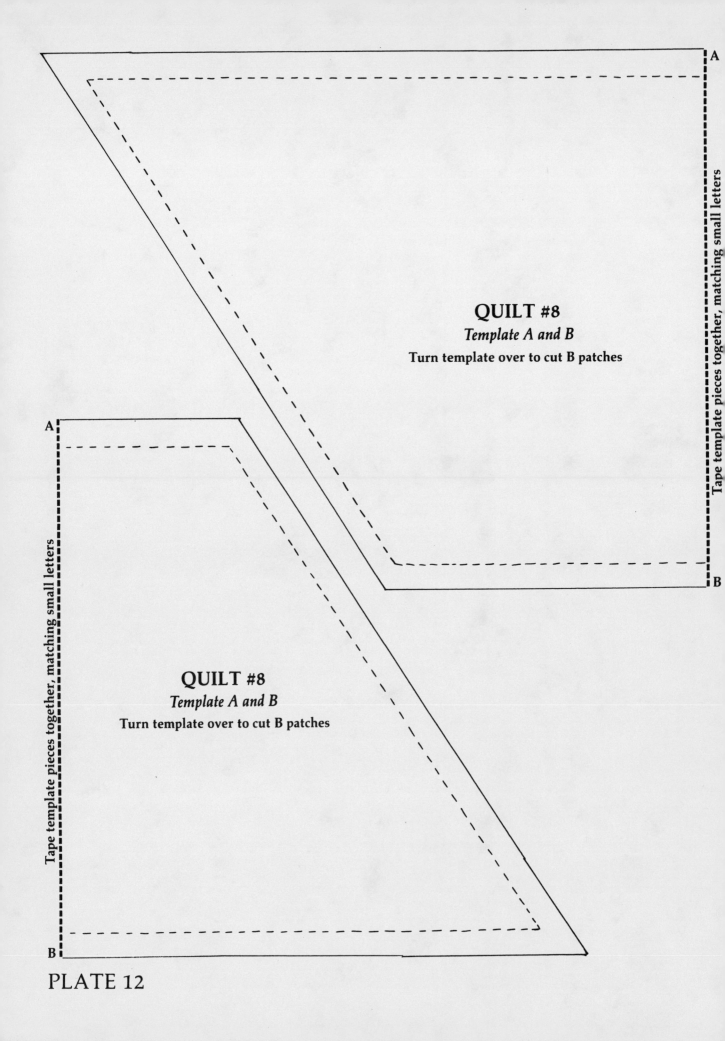

A

QUILT #8
Template A and B
Turn template over to cut B patches

A

QUILT #8
Template A and B
Turn template over to cut B patches

B

B

PLATE 12

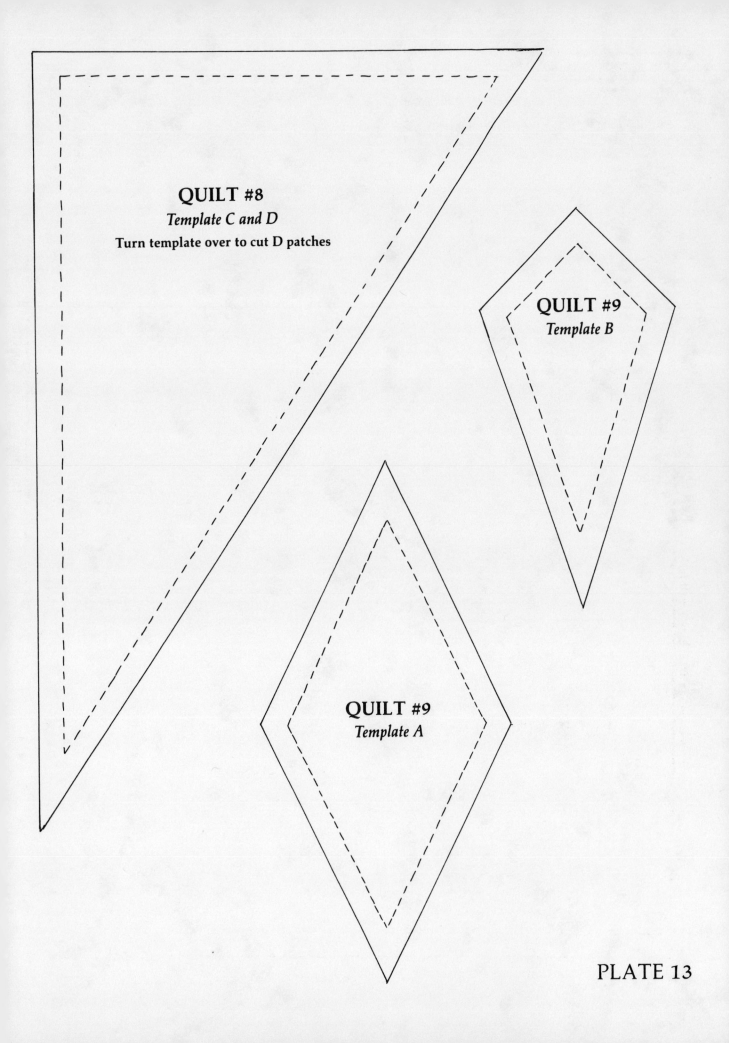

QUILT #8
Template C and D
Turn template over to cut D patches

QUILT #9
Template B

QUILT #9
Template A

PLATE 13

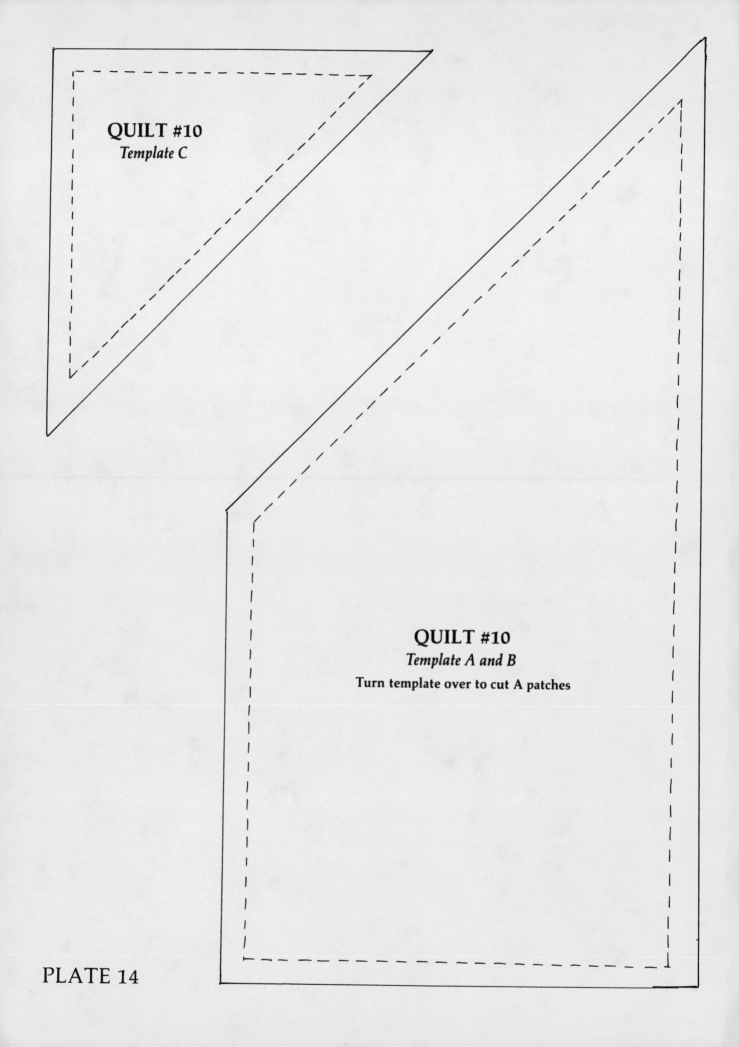

QUILT #10
Template C

QUILT #10
Template A and B
Turn template over to cut A patches

PLATE 14

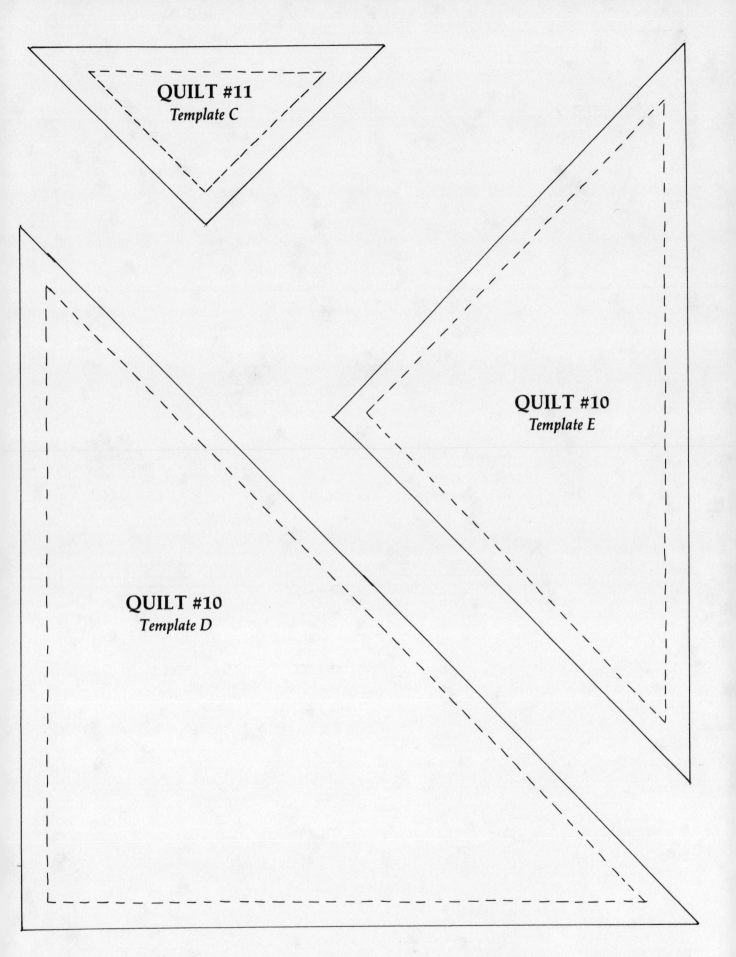

QUILT #11
Template C

QUILT #10
Template E

QUILT #10
Template D

PLATE 15